– CLEAN AS A WHISTLE –

Clean as a Whistle

Tana Reiff

Grass Roots Press

Acknowledgements

Grass Roots Press acknowledges the
financial support of the Government
of Canada for our publishing activities.

Canadä

Produced with the assistance of the
Government of Alberta through
the Alberta Media Fund.

Alberta⬛

Design: Lara Minja, Lime Design Inc.

Library and Archives Canada Cataloguing in Publication

Title: Clean as a whistle / Tana Reiff.
Names: Reiff, Tana, author.
Series: Reiff, Tana. Working for myself.
Description: Series statement: Working for myself | Originally published:
Belmont, CA : Lake Education, ©1994.
Identifiers: Canadiana 20200240463 | ISBN 9781771533539 (softcover)
Subjects: LCSH: Readers for new literates.
Classification: LCC PE1126.N43 R44454 2020 | DDC 428.6/2—dc23

1

Loves to Clean

"My kitchen floor looks great," Maggie said. She was sitting in the living room, watching TV and talking on the phone with her friend Liz. "I'm really happy with that new floor cleaner you told me about," Maggie went on. "The kids make such a mess. And the dog! Forget it! Of course, Roger is just as bad. He's always tracking in dirt."

"Don't be so hard on Roger," Liz said with a giggle. "He's a good guy. He always comes through for you. Like my boyfriend Kip. He sure surprises me sometimes."

Just then, the back door slammed.

"Nick must be home," Maggie told Liz. "I'm sure that boy will be looking for something to eat. Talk to you soon, Liz."

Nick, her 13-year-old son, walked into the living room.

"I'm hungry," said Nick. "Is there anything to eat around here?"

"You know better than to ask that question," Maggie said. "Go look in the kitchen. There's plenty to choose from. Where were you?"

"Over at Liam's house," said the boy.

"Oh, yes, the new boy. Is their house nice?" Maggie asked. She walked into the kitchen with him.

"Mom, is that all you think about? What someone's house looks like?" Nick asked. "Yes, it's a nice place—really bright and shiny."

"I made some oatmeal cookies this morning," Maggie said, changing the subject. "Want some?"

"Of course!" said Nick.

"See, I think about things besides nice, clean houses," Maggie said. "I think about food for my family."

Nick grabbed some cookies and sat down at the kitchen table. "How about a glass of milk?" he asked his mom.

"When are you going to learn to say 'please'?" Maggie asked.

"Please," Nick said, with his mouth full. "Hey, Mom, you keep talking about getting a job. Why don't you get a job cleaning houses? You love to clean."

Maggie spotted a tiny spot of dirt on the stove. She grabbed a rag to wipe it off. "What did you say?" she asked Nick.

"I said, why don't you get a job cleaning houses? Liam said his family pays someone to clean theirs."

"That's what I thought you said. I guess that might not be a bad idea. I don't know. I'm so busy just keeping my *own* house clean."

"This house is clean as a whistle," Nick said. "Why, this floor is clean enough to eat off of."

He dropped a cookie on the floor. Then he got down on his hands and knees and ate it.

"What are you *doing*?" Maggie yelled. "I just washed that floor!" She grabbed the rag to clean up the cookie crumbs. But before she could do that, the dog came in and licked the spot.

Nick started laughing. "Oh, Mom!" he said. Then he picked up his phone and started walking toward the living room.

"Don't you dare take cookies with you," said Maggie. "I don't want any crumbs in the rest of the house. I worked all day getting this place clean."

Nick shook his head as he walked away from his mother's voice. She was a great mom. He loved her more than anything. But sometimes he thought she was a bit too much.

In a minute, he was back in the kitchen. "Hey, Mom, I checked out a local jobs site for you. Look at this job," he said, pointing to his phone.

Maggie moved closer to see it. The listing said, "Do you love to clean? We have a job for you!" There was a number to call.

"Yes," Maggie said. "I love to clean. Call me nuts, but I do."

Then she looked up at the clock on the wall. "Oh, no, it's almost 5:00," she said. "I have to pick up your brother at Scouts. Please walk the dog while I get Noah. And can you write down that number for me?"

She grabbed her coat and was off like the wind.

Late that night, the housecleaning job popped into Maggie's head. She liked the sound of it.

The next morning, she called the number. By the end of the day, Maggie was an employee of the House So Clean Cleaning Service.

2

Cleaning Every Day

"So far, so good," Maggie said to Liz on the phone. "I've been working for House So Clean for, what—two weeks now? I'm telling you, it's hard to believe how some people live. Some houses look like they haven't been cleaned since the day they were built."

Liz laughed. "That's because Maggie Watson never cleaned them," she said. "The day you showed up was their lucky day."

"Don't get me wrong," Maggie said. "I still love to clean. But those houses really make me work." She was making dinner as she talked on speaker phone.

"Maybe *I* should think about getting a job, too," Liz said. "Anyway, I've got to run. Have a good night."

"You too," said Maggie. "Talk to you later. Oh, before you go, did you watch the talk shows today? What did I miss?"

"Yeah," said Liz. "They were funny today. Some crazy people. Big stars, too."

"I sure miss daytime talk shows, since I went back to work," said Maggie.

"Why don't you record them and watch them when you get home?" Liz asked.

"Good idea," said Maggie. "Except I forget how. And then I'd have to find the time to watch what I record. Working full time isn't easy, you know. Not when you have more housework to do when you get home."

"I'm sure it's hard," Liz said. "I'll show you how to record shows again when I come over. See you soon."

"See you," said Maggie.

The minute Maggie got off the phone, Roger came into the room. "How was work today?" he asked her. Roger worked nights, so he was home during the day.

"You know me. I like to clean," said Maggie. "But get this! They tell me I'm still in training. Me, in training! As if I don't already know what I'm doing. What a laugh! No one cleans like I do. *No one.*"

Maggie snorted. "They are training me to do things the way the crew leader says. But I know I clean ten times better than she does."

"I believe you," said Roger.

"She tells me to vacuum first and dust second. Everyone knows it makes more sense to dust first, vacuum second. I could teach *her* plenty about how to clean a house!"

As they talked, Maggie got out the vacuum cleaner. "I can hardly keep up with things around here," she said. She quickly ran the sweeper across the living room.

"What about dinner?" Roger asked. "Should I whip something up?"

"Dinner is already in the oven," Maggie said.

"See, you're keeping up with everything just fine," Roger told her. "I wish we could bottle up your energy and sell it. We could make a lot of money!"

"Let's see how I'm doing after a few more months," Maggie said, laughing.

Maggie surprised herself, though. She was no worse for wear as the months went on. She got to the office at 7:30 every morning. There, the boss gave each crew a list of the day's work. A two-person crew did two or three homes a day. A three-person crew did three or four. Maggie was usually on a three-person crew.

Each crew took a company van, packed with cleaning supplies. They had rags, dusters, mops, buckets, a vacuum cleaner, and a handheld vacuum for steps and small spaces.

Then off they went. The women and men laughed and joked in the van. But as soon as they walked into a customer's home, they got right to work. Part of the crew did the wet work: cleaning the kitchens and bathrooms. Part of the crew did the dry work: dusting and sweeping the other rooms. Each crew worked for eight hours. They ate lunch in the van, between homes.

"Come on, Maggie!" the crew leader would shout from the van after a job. Often, Maggie was still in the house, looking for anything they missed or wiping off a spot on a mirror.

"I'm coming!" Maggie would call out.

"We have a tight schedule!" the crew leader would yell back at Maggie.

This happened over and over again. Maggie had to have everything just right. Spotless. Perfect. She was the last one to leave every home her crew cleaned.

So the crew leader put Maggie in charge of inspecting and locking up. At most homes, all she had to do was close the door. But other places had alarm systems, and not all alarms were the same.

At some houses, to set the alarm, she had to punch numbers into a little box on the wall inside. Then she had 45 seconds to get out or the alarm would go off. She always made it out in time. Until she didn't.

That day, Maggie punched in the numbers. Then she grabbed the mop in one hand and a bucket in the other and headed out. She set the mop against the wall before she opened the door.

But the mop slipped and fell. Maggie bent down to pick it up. She knew there wasn't much time left to get out. She reached for the door again. She stepped out. But her foot caught on the rug. As the heavy door slammed behind her, her hand got caught in it. She cried out in pain.

Maggie pulled out her hand and ran to the car, carrying the mop and bucket. Then she looked down. Her fingers were bleeding. She had left a trail of red dots behind her all the way from the house.

3

On Her Own

The crew leader drove Maggie to the doctor. After the doctor's visit, the crew leader took Maggie back to the office.

"I can't believe you hurt yourself like that," said the boss.

"Well, I sure didn't do it on purpose," Maggie said.

"You should have been more careful," the boss said. "What did the doctor say about your hand?"

"He said that there are no broken bones," Maggie said. "But it's badly hurt." She showed the woman her wrapped-up hand. "The doctor said not to use my hand for a week."

"So you'll be out of work for a *week*?" the woman said angrily. "What am I supposed to do?"

"Well, I don't know," Maggie said. "I'll be back in a week. I'll be fine." Then she walked out without another word.

As soon as Maggie got home, she called her friend Liz.

"That does it!" Maggie told her friend. "I do a better job than any two of those people together. And I'm tired of taking orders from that boss."

"What are you going to do—quit?" Liz asked.

"Yes, I'm going to quit," Maggie said. "But I'm not going to stop working. I've made up my mind. I want to start my own cleaning service."

"Well, well! That's a great idea, Maggie!" said Liz.

"Just one thing," Maggie went on. "I want *you* to come in on it with me. What do you say?"

Liz did need a job. She couldn't think of a better idea. It would be fun to work with her friend Maggie. But she had a lot of questions.

"Why don't you come over for lunch?" said Maggie. "If you can help me make it. My hand is killing me. We'll talk."

And did they talk! The two women sat at Maggie's kitchen table all afternoon. It took Maggie only 15 minutes to talk Liz into going into business with her. After that, they talked about all kinds of other things. How would they get customers? What would they do about a van or SUV? What was the best cleaner for wood floors? Liz took notes on everything they talked about.

Just then, Nick and Noah burst in the back door at the same time. Maggie jumped up and reached for the fruit bowl. She set it on the counter for them. Then she turned to Liz and smiled. "These two boys eat like bears," she said.

Then she said, "Boys, please excuse us. We are having an important meeting here."

"Anything else we need to talk about?" Liz asked.

"Yes, one more thing," said Maggie. "What are we going to call ourselves?"

"I won't call you Mrs. Watson, if that's what you mean!" Liz said.

"No, no," Maggie said with a laugh. "I mean, what will we call the business? You know—like 'M and L Cleaning Service,' or whatever."

"Plain old letters aren't all that interesting," said Liz.

"How about 'Clean as a Whistle'?" Nick butted in. "I always say this house is as clean as a whistle."

"What in the world does that mean—'clean as a whistle'?" Liz asked.

"It means very, very clean," said Nick.

"I like it!" said Maggie.

"Yeah, sounds good, right?" said Nick as he headed to the living room. "Your business is really coming together."

"We'll have to register the name," said Liz. "I'll look into that." She wrote *Register name* on her to-do list.

"Oh, I just thought of something else," Maggie said. "House So Clean has company liability insurance. The workers are bonded. Should we do that?"

Liz nodded. "That means both the company and the workers are covered if they break anything or run over someone's dog or something." Then Liz wrote *Liability insurance* and *Bonding* on her list.

"Liz, you know more about running a business than I do," said Maggie. "I'm glad we're doing this together."

"Well, you know more about cleaning than I do," said Liz. "I think the two of us will make a great team. Hey, I have to go. How did it get so late?"

"Wait!" said Maggie. "Show me how to record a TV show. I'm getting behind on my TV friends. I don't want to miss anything."

"Who do you know on TV?" Noah, who was 10, asked.

"Oh, never mind," said Maggie. "Let's just say I think of them as friends. I haven't seen much of them since I went back to work."

Maggie watched closely as Liz showed her how to record her shows. Liz had shown her how to do it many times before. But somehow Maggie always forgot. In many ways, the two friends were very different types of people.

As the women said good-bye, they agreed to get together again the next day. They couldn't start a business in just one afternoon.

4

Getting Off the Ground

The next day, Maggie and Liz got together at Liz's apartment. Together, they filled out forms online. They bought liability insurance and bonding. They applied for a business license.

But there was a problem with registering the name. "Clean as a Whistle" was taken.

"Let's just call our business 'Maggie & Liz Cleaning Service,'" said Maggie.

"I like that," said Liz. "It has a nice ring to it. It tells people it's us. No fake name."

So they registered Maggie & Liz Cleaning Service.

"How are we going to pay for all this?" Maggie asked. "We'll need equipment and supplies. We'll need money to get started, won't we?"

"You're right," said Liz. "We need work—and soon. I have an idea for how we can get started."

"Talk to me," Maggie said.

"We'll call our friends," Liz began. "We need people who live in different kinds of places. Big house. Small house. Apartment. Two floors. One floor. With kids. Without kids. With a pet. Without a pet. Whatever. We'll tell them we'll clean their places for nothing."

"*What?* I thought we were trying to *make* money," Maggie broke in.

"Hold on," said Liz. "We'll do each place one time. As we work, we'll take notes. We'll write down how long it takes to do each kind of place. That will help us work out our prices."

"I get it," said Maggie. "And then our friends might want to pay us to keep coming back!"

"You've got the picture," said Liz. "And then they'll tell *their* friends what a great job we did."

"Then maybe their friends will call us," Maggie said.

"And maybe before we know it we will have all the customers we can handle," Liz said.

They started calling people right away. They quickly lined up four friends who were only too happy to have their homes cleaned for free. Maggie booked those jobs for two weeks later. By that time, her hand would be better. The insurance, business license, and name registration would be in place.

She also wanted to work one more week at House So Clean. She wanted to take notes and write down the names of the cleaning supplies.

That next week was really busy. Maggie's hand was better and she worked every day for House So Clean. Then she quit the job.

The week after that, it was time to go shopping. Both Maggie and Liz loved shopping, even if it was for cleaning supplies.

They went to a cleaning supply store. It was only for people in the business of cleaning, not for just anyone. They could have bought any of the supplies online. But they wanted to see things and try them out.

"OK," said Maggie to the salesperson. "This brand does a good job cleaning floors. Now let me see how that other brand works."

The salesperson showed Maggie how the second cleaner worked.

"OK," Maggie said. "Now let's see how other brands work when you use a different mop."

Liz rolled her eyes. "That's our Maggie!" she said to the salesperson.

The salesperson showed how each mop worked. Maggie got down on her hands and knees and looked at the floor close up.

"I don't see much difference between the different cleaners and mops," Liz said.

"I don't either," said Maggie, getting up from the floor.

"We sell only the best products," the salesperson said.

"I want to try them myself," Maggie said. She grabbed a mop and bucket and started to clean the store's floor. She used different cleaners and different mops on each part. When the whole floor was dry, she ran a finger over each part she had cleaned. Then she picked out the cleaners and mops that seemed to work best.

"Of course, floors are made differently," said the salesperson. "You should have the right cleaner for each *type* of floor. And some people only want 'green' cleaning supplies. You know, without bad chemicals in them."

"Right you are," said Maggie. She picked out five different floor cleaners for different purposes and people.

Then she looked at dozens of bathroom cleaners, window cleaners, and dusters. She studied all the labels.

"We don't need dust cloths yet," she whispered to Liz. "I have a pile of old cloth diapers at home. Believe me, they are the best, best, best."

At last, Maggie finished making her choices. Liz spoke to the salesperson. "What kind of price can you give us on these products?" she asked.

The salesperson handed Liz a price list. She marked the products they had chosen. She was ready to place an order. But Maggie whispered, "We haven't been to that other cleaning supply store yet. We should compare their prices."

So the next afternoon they drove across town. They went through the whole show all over again. They got a price list from the second store. Then they went home to order the best products at the best prices from each store.

The next afternoon, Maggie and Liz put up a sign at the grocery store. The day after that, they placed an ad in the pennysaver paper.

"We are ready to roll!" Liz said.

"What about a vacuum cleaner?" Maggie asked. "A nice big sweeper like House So Clean has. I guess that would cost a lot, wouldn't it?"

"A *lot*," Liz told her. "A vacuum will have to wait."

"We could use our own, I guess," Maggie said with a sigh.

"We can use our customers' vacuums for now," said Liz. "While we are cleaning their houses for free."

"Good idea. You're so smart," Maggie told her friend.

Monday morning, bright and early, Maggie and Liz were on the road. Their first stop was the home of their friend Inga, on Berry Lane. Together, they cleaned Inga's house from top to bottom. Then they moved on to the rest of the homes on their list.

As they worked, Liz did what she called a "time and motion study." She counted the number of rooms in each house they cleaned. She wrote down the size of each room. She wrote down how long it took to clean each room. She added up the time it took to clean the whole house. She noted whether they had kids and pets. Then she added in how long it took to drive there. At the end of the week, they could use the time and motion study to decide what their prices should be.

Maggie took notes in her head. She remembered where she had plugged in the vacuum in each room. She remembered how easy or hard each type of rug and carpet was to vacuum. She remembered which supplies she had used for which jobs.

Maggie & Liz Cleaning Service was off and running.

5

Word of Mouth

It was no surprise when Inga called Maggie & Liz Cleaning Service to clean again. "You two did a great job," she said. "Can you come every other Friday? Just give me a price."

"Sure," said Liz. "What time of day do you want us to come?"

Inga wanted them to clean in the morning, while she was home. She wanted to be there while they worked.

Liz didn't mind that Inga was there that Friday. But Maggie didn't like it. She didn't like Inga looking over her shoulder.

"Did you get this, Maggie?" Inga would say, pointing to the woodwork above a door. "Did you get that?" she would say, pointing under the sofa.

"Why does she have to be here when we clean?" Maggie asked Liz as they were leaving.

"It's *her* house," said Liz. "And remember, she's paying us now."

"Right, right," Maggie said. "Here's an idea. How about if I do all the wet cleaning and you do the dry? You know, you stick to the dusting and sweeping. I stick to the kitchen and bathrooms. I'm better at wet cleaning. And maybe Inga won't want to walk on wet floors to inspect my work. That woman gets on my nerves!"

"Fine," said Liz. "And we can help each other if one job is bigger than the other."

So, from then on, that's how they split up the work.

One day, Inga's neighbor called. "How much would you charge to clean my house every other week?" Mrs. Belson asked. "I'm a senior, you know. I can't keep up with things like I used to."

Liz said that she and Maggie would stop by and give her a price.

Mrs. Belson also lived on Berry Lane, across the street from Inga. Her house was very different from Inga's, however. Inga's house was open and simple inside. Mrs. Belson's house was packed with stuff from 80 years of living.

There were pictures of all of her four children, eight grandchildren, and three little great-grandchildren. There were knick-knacks everywhere. Her lovely old china dolls were set up on a shelf in the living room.

Maggie and Liz took one look at the place and then looked at each other. "This house is going to take *much* longer to clean than Inga's," Maggie whispered to Liz. "Look at all this stuff!"

Liz took notes as they walked from room to room. Then she worked out a price and gave it to Mrs. Belson.

"That's more than you charge Inga," said Mrs. Belson. "And her house is bigger."

"But you have more in your house to clean, Mrs. Belson," Liz explained kindly.

"I suppose you're right about that," said Mrs. Belson, looking around.

"We want to do a good job for you," Maggie added. "Nothing but the best, we always say!"

"Well, I know you do a good job for Inga," said Mrs. Belson.

So she scheduled Maggie and Liz for every other Friday, right after Inga.

Not long after that, another of Inga's neighbors, Mr. Engle, booked cleaning. Every other Friday was now full. And all of those houses were right there on Berry Lane.

After a few weeks, Maggie and Liz noticed something. They saw that cleaning the three homes on Berry Lane was taking less time.

"I should have thought of that!" said Liz. "Once we've cleaned a place a few times, we know our way around. It goes faster."

"Right!" Maggie said. "And it's easier to *keep* a place clean than to start from scratch."

"We must remember that when we work out a price," said Liz. "The first time should cost more. After that, the price can be lower."

Even so, they always spent a lot of time at Mrs. Belson's house. More than they were paid for.

Such as the day Mrs. Belson asked them to change a light bulb. Changing light bulbs was not part of the job. But Maggie didn't have the heart to say no. She said, "Sure. As long as we're here, we might as well."

Or Mrs. Belson would ask them to do a little extra cleaning. "Would you pull out the refrigerator and clean back there?" she would ask. "Don't forget to wash my baseboards! And please don't miss any of my china dolls. Every one of them needs to be carefully dusted with a clean duster."

Maggie and Liz always seemed to be doing more for Mrs. Belson than their other customers. They also listened to Mrs. Belson talk. She talked the whole time they were in her house. And sometimes she begged them to stay for lunch. She was a sweet, lonely person. They couldn't turn her down.

"She's had a long life," said Maggie one day in the car. "I think I've heard her whole life story. I feel like I know every one of her kids and grandkids and great-grandkids."

"I know what you mean," Liz said. "I don't really mind listening to her talk. Changing a light bulb is no big deal. And it's nice of her to give us lunch. But some of those extra jobs are pretty big. They're more like spring and fall housecleaning. I think we should charge extra."

Maggie didn't want to do that, but she went along with Liz. So they asked Mrs. Belson if she would like to sign up for spring and fall housecleaning. That would take all day, twice a year. It would cost more than regular cleaning.

Mrs. Belson didn't want to spend the extra money. But she understood that Maggie & Liz Cleaning Service was a business. She had done spring and fall housecleaning all her life. She knew it was a big job. And she knew she wanted it done. So she signed up. Mrs. Belson's house would be clean as a whistle all year long.

6

Feeling Pain

"Up, down, all around!" Maggie sang as she cleaned. "You really *do* like to clean, don't you?" Liz said, laughing.

"Sure, I have always loved to clean," Maggie said. "I still enjoy it—even now that it's a business."

"What I like best is being on our own," said Liz.

Maggie & Liz Cleaning Service had full-time work nearly every week now. One person told another about them. Some jobs came from the ads in the pennysaver paper. A few more came from the sign at the grocery store. Most came from word of mouth.

Liz talked with all the new customers. She explained the difference between regular cleaning and other jobs, like window washing. And how cleaning a house once a week didn't take as long as cleaning it every other week. Homes without pets didn't get too dirty in just one week. Especially if it had been cleaned right the first time.

These full weeks of cleaning were hard work for Maggie and Liz. Their backs and knees felt it. So, more than ever, Maggie enjoyed sitting down and watching the talk shows she recorded during the day.

One evening, after one of the shows, she started to get out of her chair. She was halfway up when she fell back down into it. Her body was *tired*.

"I must be getting old," she said.

"Maybe you're *feeling* old, Mom," said her son Nick. "You are working really hard. But I think you're looking more fit."

"Well, I *have* lost a few pounds," Maggie said. "All this extra work is good exercise, I guess."

"The extra money's not bad either!" Roger said. He was getting ready to head to work.

"We do have our bad days sometimes," said Maggie. "Like today."

"What happened?" Roger asked.

Maggie told the story. About how she always wanted to stay at a house and keep cleaning until it was perfect. Liz kept her on the move. She made sure they didn't spend too much time at any one place. Today, they had lost a lot of time.

First, Maggie's car broke down. Maggie and Liz moved everything into Liz's car while they waited an hour for a tow truck.

At last, they got to Berry Lane—first Inga's house, then Mrs. Belson's. Mrs. Belson was usually at home when they cleaned. Today she had called to say she would be visiting her daughter.

"Can you leave us the key?" Liz had asked her.

"Oh my, no," Mrs. Belson said. "It's not that I don't trust you girls. But what if the wrong person found it? I'll wait until you get here to let you in."

However, when Maggie and Liz finally got there, no one was home. The door was locked. They asked Inga if Mrs. Belson had left her a key. She hadn't. They asked three other neighbors. No one had Mrs. Belson's key. So they couldn't get into the house. Maggie and Liz had gone there for nothing.

Then they went on to Mr. Engle's house. Like a lot of customers, he had an alarm system. This one's box was outside, beside the door. Maggie and Liz had the code.

But after Liz pressed the buttons, the door did not open. She tried again. Still, the door was locked.

"Let me try!" Maggie said.

It was the third try. After the third try, the alarm went off. It was loud. Really, really loud. It hurt their ears. The noise was like ten smoke alarms all going off at once.

Maggie and Liz ran out onto the front lawn. Even that didn't help much with the noise. Neighbors came out of their houses to see what was wrong. Everyone held their hands over their ears.

In a few minutes, a car pulled up. A man in a uniform jumped out and ran toward the house. "I'm in charge of answering these alarms," he said. He knew what to do. He quickly turned off the alarm, then came over to Maggie and Liz.

"We're the cleaning people," Liz explained. "We had the code, but it didn't work today."

The man let Maggie and Liz into the house and called Mr. Engle at work.

"Tell my great cleaning people I'm really sorry," said Mr. Engle. "I changed the code and forgot to tell them."

Maggie turned to Liz. "My ears are ringing like a fire truck on its way to a fire. I just *hate* those house alarms!"

Their ears were still ringing as Maggie and Liz cleaned Mr. Engle's house. It died down a little as they drove home. But even as Maggie watched TV that night, she could still hear Mr. Engle's alarm ringing in her head.

7

Help Wanted

Liz gave every customer a note. It said, "If you change your alarm code or house key, please tell us right away. If we cannot get into your home, you will be charged the regular cleaning fee."

But other surprises happened, too. There was the day Liz got sick. "What am I going to do?" Maggie asked Liz on the phone. She sounded worried.

"You just have to clean without me today," Liz told her. "We can never tell a customer we can't come."

"Unless we're both dead, right?" said Maggie.

"Right," Liz said, laughing. "I'm sorry, but you're just going to have to do three houses yourself today."

"I'll be working till midnight if I work alone!" Maggie said.

"Can you find someone to help you? How about Roger? He's off during the day now, isn't he?"

"Roger?!" Maggie cried out. "Excuse me while I die laughing. Are you talking about the man who drops his socks wherever he takes them off? You want me to ask

the man who doesn't know which is the business end of a mop?"

"Anyone can run a vacuum," said Liz. "Even Roger. Hey, let me tell you a secret. Remember when Nick was born? Well, Roger vacuumed your house while you were in the hospital. You thought I did it. He didn't want you to know because he didn't want to keep doing it."

"Really?" said Maggie. "Well . . . OK, I'll ask him. Maybe he won't mind so much when he sees the super new vacuum we saved up to buy. He loves big machines."

At first, Roger said he had to sleep. Even though this was his night off work. Then he said he had to cut the grass.

"How many excuses can you come up with?" Maggie said. "It's only one day."

"I'm not making excuses," Roger said. But he knew that he *was* making excuses. "Well, all right. I'll run the vacuum. The heck with sleeping."

So Roger went along with Maggie. Together, they finished all three houses in good time.

After he ran the big vacuum at the first house, Roger said, "This is hard work. I had no idea!"

After the second house, Roger said, "Liz was right. Anyone can run a vacuum."

After the third house, Roger said, "This is kind of fun. Your brand-new vacuum cleaner works great, doesn't it?"

At that last house, the customer asked Roger if he cleaned carpets.

"I believe I just cleaned your carpet, ma'am," Roger said.

"No, I mean steam cleaning," said the woman.

Roger was ready to say, "No, we don't steam clean carpets." Then he had a thought. He could rent a steam cleaner. "Why, yes, we steam clean carpets," he said. "When would you like us to do it for you?"

The woman asked him to do it next Thursday. "That way, it will be clean and dry for the weekend," she said to Roger.

When Thursday rolled around, Roger stopped to rent a steam cleaner at the grocery store. He also had to buy a special carpet soap.

"I've never done this before," he said to the clerk. "Can you tell me a little bit about it?"

"The directions are on the machine," said the clerk.

"OK," Roger said. "I can see I won't get any help here."

He carried the steam cleaner to the car. Then he tried to read the directions. He could read the words, but he wasn't sure he understood them. "I'll figure it out," he told himself.

Lucky Roger! The customer knew how the steam cleaner worked. Roger tried to act as if he done it a hundred times before. But he let the woman show him what to do.

Roger cleaned carpets in two rooms. It took half a day. But when he was finished, those carpets were *clean*.

And he had made a nice bit of money for Maggie & Liz Cleaning Service.

"You can start telling people that we clean carpets," Roger told Maggie when she got home.

Maggie was surprised. Who would have thought that Roger would enjoy cleaning carpets? "I'll get you carpet work if you start picking up your socks," she said with a laugh.

Maggie told Liz and they both got the word out. Before long, Roger was doing two or three carpet jobs each week.

Then, about a month later, Roger came home with bad news. It had been hard enough when he got pushed to night work. Now the night shift was cut. Roger was laid off.

Somehow it didn't seem as bad as it could have been. There were always carpets to clean. And Roger was ready to clean them.

8

Everyone Has Windows

More and more customers began asking about window washing.

"I don't know what to tell people," Maggie told Liz. "If I spend any time on a ladder, I just know I'll fall and break a bone. And I only have one husband to give to the business."

"I don't like to say no to paying work," Liz said. "It seems a shame to turn down the extra money."

"Well, how about your boyfriend?" Maggie asked.

"Kip could use some work," said Maggie. "He's been out of a job for a while now."

"Well, you never know till you ask," Maggie said.

So Liz asked Kip. As it turned out, he was happy to try window washing. He hadn't done that kind of work before, so he looked up what to do. Maggie & Liz Cleaning Service bought him some window-washing supplies.

At first, all of the window washing came from Maggie & Liz Cleaning Service customers. But Kip really enjoyed the work. He liked the squeak of the squeegee down the glass. He liked the shine of a squeaky clean window on a sunny day.

Word spread about Kip's great work. Soon they were adding new customers to their window-cleaning service. They were getting busier and busier.

Now Maggie and Liz were up to four houses a day. They had a list of tasks to do at each place. They checked off each task as they went. They worked fast and well together. But four houses a day was a lot for a two-person crew. And the calls kept coming in.

"What would you think of taking on another person?" Liz asked one day.

"I like working with *you*," Maggie said. "And we've become even better friends over the past year and half. But I don't know about being a *boss*. It just wouldn't feel right."

"You know how I feel about turning down work," Liz said.

"I know you don't like to turn down work," said Maggie. "But I vote to stay small. We already have Roger doing carpets. We have Kip doing windows. That's enough. I don't want to run a big company here."

"*I* vote to grow," Liz said. "I can see big things ahead in this business."

"Then I guess we have a problem," said Maggie. "This is the first time we haven't seen eye to eye."

Maggie and Liz didn't talk much the rest of the day. They weren't used to being upset with each other. But today, they were both feeling a little angry.

The next few days were not much better between the two of them. Then Liz heard something on the radio that caught her interest. It was about a group that helped small businesses start up and run.

Liz told Maggie about this free counseling service. "I think we should find out if they could help us."

"OK," said Maggie. "Let's check into it."

Liz set up a meeting. A week later, she and Maggie met their counselor. He was an older man named Web Morris. He had run an office-cleaning service for 30 years. He understood the problem that Liz and Maggie were having. To grow or not to grow?

"I always knew there was plenty of cleaning work out there," Web said about his days in the business. "Plenty of carpets, too. And every home has windows. There's just no end to what you could do. I chose to keep my business to office cleaning only. I dropped everything else as the office cleaning grew."

"That's interesting," said Liz. "I want to grow the window-cleaning side of the business. Maybe branch out more into other areas. Hire people. Grow our whole business, really."

"I want to stay small," said Maggie. "Stick to houses and carpet cleaning, with window cleaning as an add-on."

"You're saying you're happy with the way things are, Maggie?" Web asked.

"You get it," said Maggie.

"So what do you think we should do?" Liz asked Web.

"I can't tell you what to do," said Web. "But I *can* ask you questions to help you figure things out. Liz, how would you feel about going out on your own? Think about it. You could hire people to work for you and grow as large as you want."

"Without Maggie? Wow! I don't know. She's the best in the world."

"And Maggie, how about a small home-cleaning business of *your* own?" he asked.

Maggie was at a loss for words. She knew Liz was the brains of the business. Yet she had learned quite a bit about how to run a business herself. At this point, she felt pretty sure she could handle a small cleaning business of her own.

"Of course, I would send all the carpet cleaning to Roger," Liz said.

"And I would send the window washing to Kip," Maggie said.

Maggie, Liz, and Web talked for another hour. They talked about "what if" this and "what if" that.

By the time they left the office, Liz had decided what she wanted to do. So had Maggie. Liz wanted to grow. Maggie wanted to stay small. The answer to their differences was really very clear.

9

Liz and Kip

Maggie and Liz each took half of their customers. Maggie bought out Liz's share of the vacuum cleaner. Liz bought a bigger one. It was a good start for the two new businesses. And they stayed friends.

Neither of them could use the name Maggie & Liz Cleaning Service. That name no longer fit.

Maggie decided to just use her own name. No need to register that.

Liz registered her business as Maids & Windows. That clearly told what the business did: housecleaning and window washing.

Liz went back to the counselor and worked out a business plan that included Kip on windows. She got a small-business loan at the bank and bought a van. She had *Maids & Windows* painted on the sides and back of it.

She bought a laptop computer and hired a small company to build her a website. She signed up with a site for people looking for home services. The site would keep a share of any business that came out of it. She kept track of all her bookings on the laptop. She carried that computer everywhere she went.

Then Liz had to find people to work for her. She planned to hire two people. She listed the positions on a jobs website. The listing said:

> If you're looking for good, clean work, this is the job for you! Join the team at Maids & Windows. No weekends. Daytime hours are Monday–Friday and we are closed on major holidays. If you are a high-energy person interested in housecleaning work, APPLY NOW! We offer THE HIGHEST PAY FOR CLEANING IN THE AREA!

At first, only a few people applied, and they didn't look good to Liz.

"I thought a lot of people were looking for work," she said to Kip.

"Not everyone wants to clean houses," Kip told her. "That's why there's plenty of work out there for *you*."

But then more people began to apply. Liz picked three to interview. She set up video chats because she wanted to see what they looked like.

The first woman's hair was messed up. *Maybe it's the wind,* Liz said to herself. *Or maybe it doesn't mean anything.* The woman's clothes did not look very clean. She probably really needs the money, Liz thought.

Liz started asking her questions. *Why do you want to clean homes? Do you show up on time? What would you do if you broke something while you were cleaning?*

The woman couldn't give one clear answer. Liz knew she would not be hiring this person.

The second woman was older, probably around 60. She looked neat and clean and seemed very nice.

"My husband lost his job," the woman said. "We're afraid he'll never find a new one at his age. We need the money badly. Cleaning is the only thing I know how to do."

This woman seemed much more like the kind of person Liz was looking for.

The third woman was young. She had a lot of energy. And she really wanted the job.

"I had a job with a large cleaning service," said the young woman. "I know the work, and I'd like to stay in the cleaning field."

"Why did you leave?" Liz asked.

"Well ... I didn't get along with the boss," the young woman said.

Liz wondered if this woman had worked for House So Clean, so she asked. She had. She even knew Maggie.

"I don't think you'll have trouble getting along with me," Liz said.

That evening, she called Maggie to ask about the young woman. Maggie remembered her. She said the young woman was a good worker.

More people applied. But Liz decided to hire the older woman and the young woman who had worked with Maggie.

Liz took an online course on how to do payroll. She found out there was a lot to learn. Having employees meant new things to do. She didn't want to make any mistakes. In the end, she decided to pay someone to do the payroll for her.

Liz went after new business. She lined up work cleaning apartments after people moved out. She ordered business cards for customers to give to their friends. And she left her card at doors in nice neighborhoods.

Just two months later, Liz hired two more people. Every day she sent out two-person crews. She stayed behind to run the business from her home office. If someone could not come to work, she filled in on a crew herself.

Kip bought some better window-washing tools. He got a friend to help him do the work. Cleaning windows was much easier with two people working together.

A year later, Maids & Windows had become too large for Liz's apartment. She also needed more storage space. So Liz rented a small office with space in the back to store equipment and cleaning supplies.

"Just think of it! It's hard to believe. Two years ago I was keeping Maggie up to date on her daytime talk shows," she said to Kip one night. "Look at me today!"

10

Maggie and Roger

"Why are you taking a picture of that carpet?" Maggie asked Roger.

"Before and after," said Roger. "This is the 'before' picture. See how dirty it is? Then I'll take an 'after' picture when I'm done cleaning it."

"What a good idea! That's what I should do at home," Maggie said, laughing. "Take a picture after I clean, but *before* the boys get home. Then take another picture after they have been in the house for five minutes. What a difference!"

"I'm putting together pictures to show people," Roger explained. "Then they can see for themselves how great my new carpet-cleaning machine works."

Roger had his own steam cleaner now. He didn't have to rent one anymore. It was a big, powerful machine. He bought it used, but it did a great job.

Roger said that was only the first step. What he *really* wanted was a truck-mounted steam cleaner. He wouldn't have to bring it into homes. But he would have to wait a few years. That kind of equipment cost a lot of money. Besides, he would need a new truck to put it on.

For now, Roger was happy just to have his own steam cleaner. He saved a lot of money by not having to rent one. And he saved driving time because he always had the carpet cleaner in the back of his SUV.

Roger had learned a lot. Now he knew what he was doing when he walked into a home. "See that carpet?" he would say. "Looks gray-blue, right?" Then he would pull out a color chart. "I'll make you a bet. When I'm finished, your carpet will be blue, like this color. If it isn't, you'll get the job for half price."

He also told people which stains he would *not* be able to get out. People always took Roger's bet. He never lost. He even made extra money by putting on a stain guard after a cleaning.

Roger did not stay on as part of Maggie's business. Instead, he started his own. He called it Roger's Carpet Cleaning. "Nice, friendly name," he said. He ordered his own business cards.

And, being a carpet cleaner, he tracked much less dirt into the house these days. He now understood all about clean floors. That made Maggie happy.

Meanwhile, Maggie had everything just the way she wanted it. She cleaned two or three houses a day, four days a week, all by herself. Then she had a whole day to clean her own house, cook, or watch her talk shows. She was also home for the boys every day after school and could drive them anywhere they needed to go.

"I love to clean," she would say. "But it's not worth dying for!" That is why she stuck to cleaning only houses and apartments. And sent all the heavy work to Liz.

Of course, Maggie needed to be on the lookout for new business, too. But she didn't want to make a business card or buy any ads. She liked getting work through word of mouth—one happy customer telling someone else. If she had an open time, she told her customers about it in case they knew anyone who might fill it.

If someone called, she would visit the home, look around, and give the person a price for the job. She signed people up for cleaning service once a week, once every two weeks, or once a month. The money both she and Roger made was enough for the family to live on.

One customer that she kept from the early days was Mrs. Belson. Maggie ate lunch with her older friend every Friday. This went on for three more years.

Then one day, Mrs. Belson told Maggie she would be moving from Berry Lane. She had decided to move to a small apartment at a place only for seniors. Cleaning would be done for her there. She planned to give away or sell most of her things. Her children and grandchildren had no interest in most of it.

"I want you to have something of mine," Mrs. Belson said to Maggie. The old woman took a beautiful china doll from the shelf in the living room. "Take this," she said to Maggie. "Please. Think of me when you look at it."

Maggie was touched. All she could say was, "I will. Thank you." But she was also thinking of the past. She remembered the hundreds of times she had dusted that doll. The hundreds of times she had dusted *all* of Mrs. Belson's china dolls. Most of all, she would remember Mrs. Belson.

Yes, Maggie Watson loved to clean. Even an old woman's china dolls.

She thought about the last few years. Some things change—many parts of Maggie's life had changed. But some things, like her love of cleaning, stayed the same. And that was a love that Maggie never wanted to change.